# Nuclear, Biological and Chemical Warfare In-Home Shelter Plan

**By   Malcolm McDaniel**

**BS Environmental Engineering**

**This assembly and usage procedure is protected by patent Number 6,666,910 B2**

**©2000**

I would like to offer a special thank you
to Dr. Paul R. Bienkowski, Mr. Todd Brethauer,
William L. Burkhart MD and Ronald J. Estes MD,
for freely offering their valuable advice.

# Forward

Have you ever imagined what you would do if a voice on your radio or TV announced a nuclear, biological, or chemical (NBC) warfare attack had made the air outside your house deadly? Would you panic, knowing that you might soon have to watch your children suffer a horrible death or illness? Or would you be calm knowing that you already had a defensive game plan that could save you and your family?

As recently as 25 years ago the notion that average persons could isolate themselves in a single room of their house while providing for all of their metabolic needs such as clean air, water, food, and waste containment for days at a time was nonsensical. But that was largely before plastics. Today, thanks to the proliferation of plastics, such an endeavor is totally possible, and at an astonishingly low price. Of the above metabolic needs, providing purified air has always been the most technically difficult problem to solve and until now all shelters relied on gas powered generators to run fans which forced air through filters. Today, some very simple products can be put together in such a way to produce a forced air purification system which can be powered by batteries or if necessary powered by a person.

It is the hope of this author to persuade as many people as can be persuaded that even the very modest defensive preparations for nuclear, biological, or chemical warfare described here will offer them substantial opportunities for saving the lives and health of their loved ones. In addition, the shelter plan gives simple and specific instructions on the order of a "how to" book for quickly building and then living in an in-home shelter, completely isolated and self sustainable for perhaps many days.

# Notice

The in-home shelter as presented in this document provides no protection for the radiation produced by a nuclear blast but could be used in conjunction with a blast shelter if desired. It would, however, be helpful as is to those living many miles down wind from a nuclear blast by preventing the inhalation of radioactive particles.

# Disclaimer

The following strategy was developed solely by the author without assistance or approval from any government agency and represents the author's personal beliefs. In the event of an actual disaster or attack, the information and suggestions given are not meant to supersede any instructions issued by any legally authorized government agency. Neither the author nor the publisher has tested the means, methods, procedures and strategies stated herein under actual disaster or attack conditions or for an extended period of time. Neither the author nor the publisher makes any representations or warranties, express or implied, that the means, methods, procedures and strategies stated herein will work precisely as stated herein or will prevent sickness, illness or death under actual disaster or attack conditions, and all such warranties are expressly disclaimed. The author and publisher disclaim responsibility or liability for any loss or hardship that may be incurred as a result of the use, application or misuse of any information included in *Nuclear, Biological, and Chemical Warfare In-home Shelter Plan.*

# CONTENTS

# Section 1
## Don't Assume the Worst Possible Scenario

Most of us go about our daily business never giving two seconds thought to what we would do if a nuclear, biological, or chemical attack occurred close enough to our home to affect us. Most likely this reticence to consider the matter stems from the fact that we have all been bombarded with Hollywood portrayals of agonizingly gruesome biological plagues, smoldering cities and visions of death and destruction which are simply mind numbing. The collective effect of all this conditioning is to make us believe that there is absolutely nothing we can do to protect ourselves, that we are totally at the mercy of forces we cannot control. If this were completely true then perhaps it would be best to put the whole matter out of our minds, but the truth is that not all of us face the same risks and most of us can survive these kinds of attacks, if prepared.

Before the collapse of the Soviet Union the threat of nuclear war was very different than it is today. The reality of MAD (Mutual Assured Destruction) meant that choosing to launch a nuclear missile meant the probable end of the entire world and, thankfully, no one was willing to do that. Now, with many more countries armed, it is likely that NBC attacks will be on a smaller scale and while they will be instantly deadly for those at ground zero, the total death count will depend on the extent to which people who are not at ground zero are able to protect themselves from the resulting contaminated air.

The goal of this document is to increase your chances of surviving an NBC attack by showing you how to filter radioactive particles, biological pathogens, and chemical poisons from your breathing air. There is a great deal more to be learned about NBC warfare  survival than is presented in this document and this document is only meant to be a part of a larger collection of NBC survival skills. A tremendous amount of material is available on the internet and in libraries.

### CHEMICAL WEAPONS

We have some recent experience by way of the *Middle East Gulf War which has shown that trace levels of chemical weapons can have devastating health effects for those who unknowingly breathe them. While our government has been tentative about the causal relationship between the unexplained and serious health problems among Gulf War GI's and the accidental destruction of an Iraqi bunker containing chemical weapons munitions, it has become clear that such a relationship exists.

While avoiding the details of chemical weapons technology, it's an accurate simplification to say that the fewer chemical weapons molecules are breathed into the lungs, the healthier you will be. What this means to you and your family is that if the source of chemical weapons molecules is several miles away from your home, then you have a window of time in which you can get prepared to filter out all of those molecules reaching your breathing air.  By following the instructions for constructing an in-home shelter ahead of time, and then storing the materials away in a closet,

*Operation Desert Storm, Aug.2, 1990

you and many thousands of people might be saved from death and disability.

## NUCLEAR WEAPONS

In the case of a nuclear bomb or a Chernobyl type nuclear event, the same general rules apply, except there would also be a potentially large kill zone where only an underground shelter would be able to save you from radiation sickness or death. Hopefully our government will be able to evacuate those people who should leave their homes. People who are not in these zones may have between minutes and hours in which they can get prepared to completely filter radio active fallout from the air. Just like chemical weapons molecules, the fewer particles of nuclear fallout are breathed, the better. The in-home shelter offers a significant health advantage over military respirators because it puts more inches of space between you and the particles which are emitting radiation. It could also be incorporated into a bomb shelter plan to produce a less expensive bomb shelter.

## BIOLOGICAL WEAPONS

The science of biological warfare is much more complicated than the others and consequently, it is more difficult to give specific advice about dealing with it. Generally speaking, the best way to stop a spreading plague is isolation and quarantine. In this respect, the in-home shelter could play a significant part in stopping a biological event in its tracks. If you are certain that all the members of your family or shelter party are free from disease then going into isolation or partial isolation in your shelter is obviously your best course of action. If you are not certain, then a whole host of other factors must be considered before choosing this option. The availability of medical attention and your own particular circumstances must be factored into any decision you make regarding isolation.

## VOLCANIC ERUPTIONS

A naturally occurring but devastating cataclysmic event which also has the potential to kill countless millions of people through airborne toxins and particles is the volcanic eruption. Geologists have determined that a super volcano, directly under Yellow Stone National Park did indeed kill animals as far away as 900 miles to the east by a choking rain of volcanic ash. Should such an event reoccur, having an in-home shelter with the capacity to filter particles and toxic gasses from your breathing air and meet your other metabolic needs for days could save your life.

In summary, being at ground zero of any type of surprise NBC attack would be fatal for those present, however, no one should assume that they would be at ground zero. People who are not in the kill zone of nuclear or chemical attacks or not in contact with people from an area hit with biological agents have opportunities to protect themselves from airborne toxic substances. It is even possible that the air in your country could be contaminated by wide scale NBC warfare on other continents, which might allow a window of opportunity of days in which to prepare a shelter.

# Section 2
## Preparing for Disaster

Often the most important factor determining whether a person survives a disaster is the extent to which the person has developed, in advance, a survival strategy. For example, smart people have a plan for getting out of their house during a fire. They carry a blanket in the car when they travel in snow, and they carry life jackets when boating. Having a plan before disaster strikes can be the difference between life and death. To give you an example of a missed opportunity for survival, look at the Titanic disaster. Panic and stress prevented anyone from realizing that the wooden doors on the virgin ship could be quickly removed and floated on top of unlaced and outstretched life jackets. Lying flat on top of the door surfboard style would have kept many people above water until help arrived. Clearly, even the smartest among us can't think creatively under stress.

I saw on television recently, that a company which produces prefabricated bomb shelters is doing a very good business now. Their shelters cost in the $40,000 range and 20 were shipped to DC before the new millennium. This is clearly the Cadillac of protection strategy but is available to only a very few people. At the other end of the "protection spectrum" a person could ignore the issue completely which is what most people are doing right now. I suspect the reason for this is that most people believe only an expensive bomb shelter would save their lives. This presumption is fatalistic and incorrect. For less than $200, materials can be purchased which would provide most of the same lifesaving properties.

The remainder of this manual provides the detailed directions for quickly converting a room of your house into a safe in-home shelter and instructions for living in it. Following the instructions for constructing your shelter are supply check-off lists which can be used both for purchasing the supplies you will need to sustain life and to make sure they make it into your shelter before you seal the door opening.

Briefly, you will be selecting one room in your house, preferably with only one door and one or two windows, which will be your shelter for perhaps several days. You will use duct tape and plastic to seal your room from the outside air so that the only way air can get into the room is through the air filtration system you will construct.

Your basic materials will consist of:

heavy vinyl shower curtains or 6 mil clear plastic sheeting
2-6 NBC filters plus an equal number as back ups (use organic paint respirator filters only if NBC types are totally unavailable)
a sturdy cardboard box  (between 15"X15"X15" and 24"X24"X24")

4 to 6 rolls duct tape
2 rolls packaging tape
a foot operated air pump (must have deflate capabilities)
a 12 volt DC battery operated air pump
clove oil for testing your seal

If you saw Apollo 13 then you can appreciate how they used the "stuff" on hand, including duct tape to invent what they needed to survive. With the above stuff you will be able to construct a first class air purification system. You will be able to draw fresh filtered air into your room with a foot or battery powered pump and as you are doing that you will be pressurizing your air space within, which will cause the airflow at any tiny leaks to be from inside to outside. At about 30 dollars apiece, the most expensive and hardest to get component will be the NBC (nuclear, biological, chemical) respirator filters or if you cannot find them, organic vapor paint filters which are better than nothing. Don't wait until it's too late. You can put all of your materials inside your cardboard box and store it away until you need it. If kept sealed, new filters will last for years.

**Typical Bedroom Converted
into an Isolation Room**

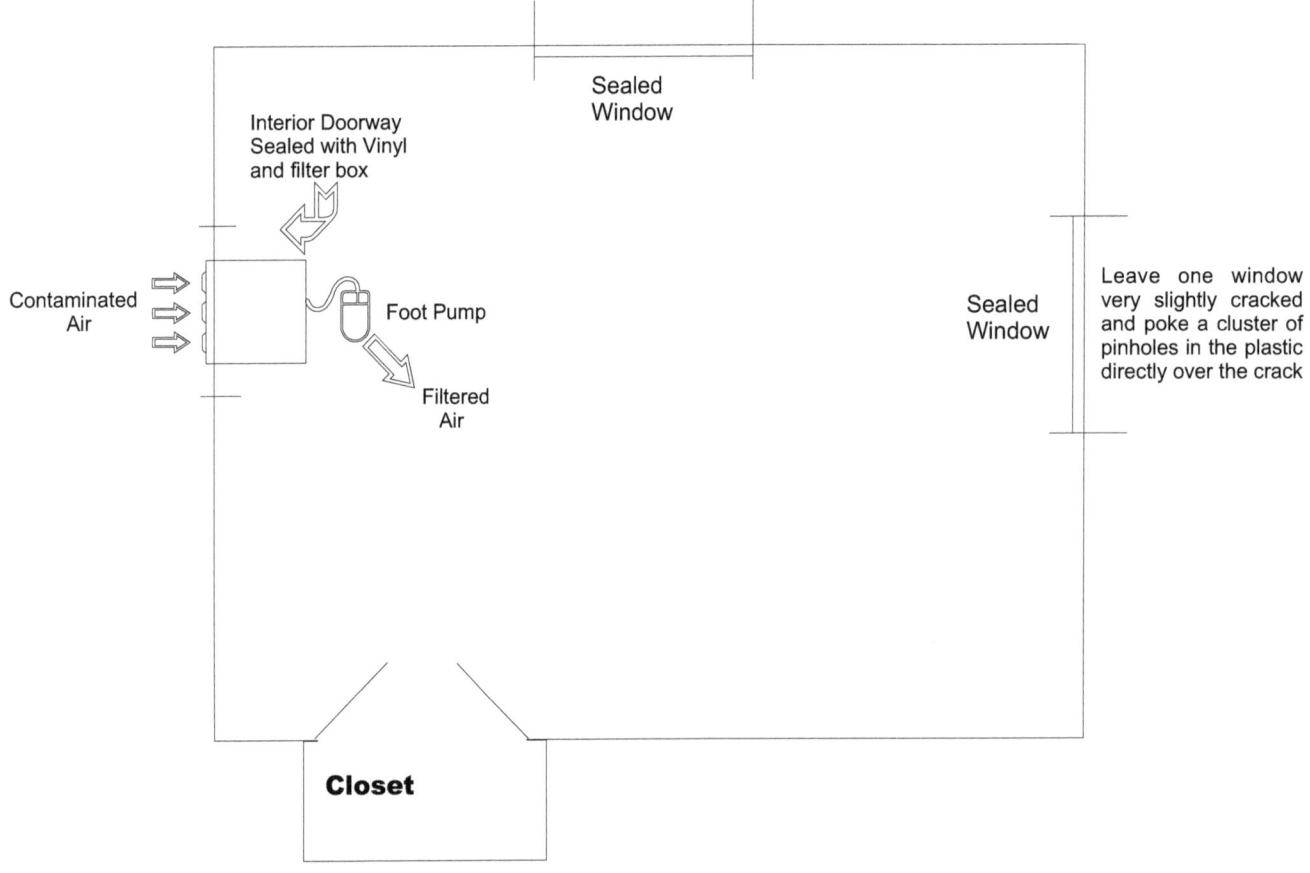

Figure 1.

# Section 3
# Assembling the Air Filter

Assembly Instructions:

The primary tools and supplies you will need to construct your air filter are Shown in photo 1.

Step 1. Gather together the following materials;

A  sturdy cardboard box (around 15"X15"X15" to 24"X24"X24")
foot pump, Sevylor model 304 shown
12 volt DC air pump (Quick-Fill by Intex shown)
plastic sheeting or heavy vinyl shower curtains
NBC filters; sealed and not expired (1 or 2 per person who will be sheltered)
organic vapor respirator filters (only use if NBC type filters are unavailable)
utility knife
duct tape
packaging tape
scissors
marking pen

Photo 1.

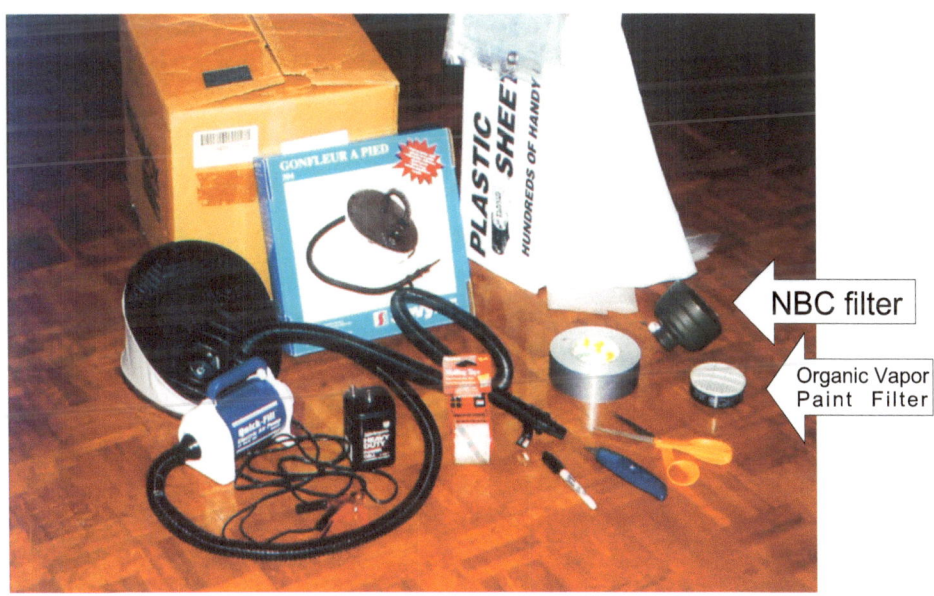

Step 2. Mark filter hole locations.

I have chosen to use 5 NBC filters to construct my air filter which will easily provide filtered air for 5 people. You will need to select a box size which will hold the number of filters you want to use, allowing one filter per person. Take the filters you will use and trace their location on the side of your box. It's better to mark and cut the holes a bit smaller than too big. Space the filters at least 2" apart and allow at least 1" between the filters and the edge of the box.

Photo 2.

Step 3. Cut holes for filters.

Using an Olfa or utility knife, carefully cut out the circles you have traced being sure not to cut the holes bigger than the filters.

Photo 3.

Step 4. Cut vinyl or polyethylene doorway cover.

Cut out a piece of clear polyethylene or vinyl plastic which is four inches wider than the doorway opening you intend to use. Cut the plastic about 6" longer than the doorway height. Lay the plastic on top of the side with the holes as shown in the photo, allowing the plastic to hang over the bottom of the box about 4." If you are using a piece of clear vinyl shower curtain and it is too short for your door opening you should use duct tape to splice on another piece of plastic to the end. Be sure that you tape over the seam on both sides of the plastic sheet. (see splice in photo 9)

Photo 4.

Step 5. Mark and cut filter openings in plastic sheeting.

Trace the outline of the holes on the clear plastic with a marking pen. While keeping the plastic sheet in place with one hand, use the utility knife to cut the plastic pizza-style as shown. Cut a 1" by 2 or 3" piece of packing tape and place over the apex of one of the triangular tabs.

Photo 5.

Step 6. Secure plastic tabs to inside of box.

Pull the point of the triangular piece through to the inside of the box and hold in place using more packaging tape. Repeat steps 5 and 6 until all the tabs are pulled to the inside of the box and taped down.

Photo 6.

Step 7. Set filters.

In this step you will place your respirator filters into the holes and seal around the edges with duct tape. If you are using military filters you will need to cut the string that is attached to both the front and back seals of the filter. If you are using organic paint respirator filters you will need to remove them from their plastic bags. Be sure to cover the front and back side of the filters with tape after you have completed your air filtration box. The reason for doing this is that the filters absorb molecules from the air even if air is not being forced through them. Each filter has the capacity to absorb only a finite number of molecules and then it is no longer effective. You don't want to reduce that capacity by exposing it to the air unnecessarily. If you would like to test your air filtration box and you are using military filters, you may remove the seals on the filters but be sure to put them back over the holes when you are finished testing.

The filters should fit snugly into the holes. Cut small pieces of duct tape and seal the crack between the filter and the box. Make sure that there are no gaps or cracks that might allow air to get into the box without going through the filters.

Photo 7.

Step 8. Seal bottom of doorway.

Before installing your air filter box you may need to remove the door from the opening.  This is easily done by removing the hinge pins. Remove the seals or tape on
the front and back holes of the filters before sealing the doorway.

Place the air filtration box filter side down in the doorway as shown. Our
demonstration shows a smooth wood floor, however if the room you choose is
carpeted you will need to pull up the carpet at least in front of the door and
maybe around the entire room. (this will be addressed later) Remove the threshold
strip if necessary. Use duct tape to tape the bottom edge of the plastic to the floor as
shown in photo 8.

Photo 8.

Step 9.  Seal around entire door.

Carefully measure and trim the plastic sheeting so as to allow for taping the remaining edges of the plastic to the floor, sides and top of the door opening. If possible, tape to the smoothest surface surrounding the door. In our example the wood trim was smoother than the drywall.

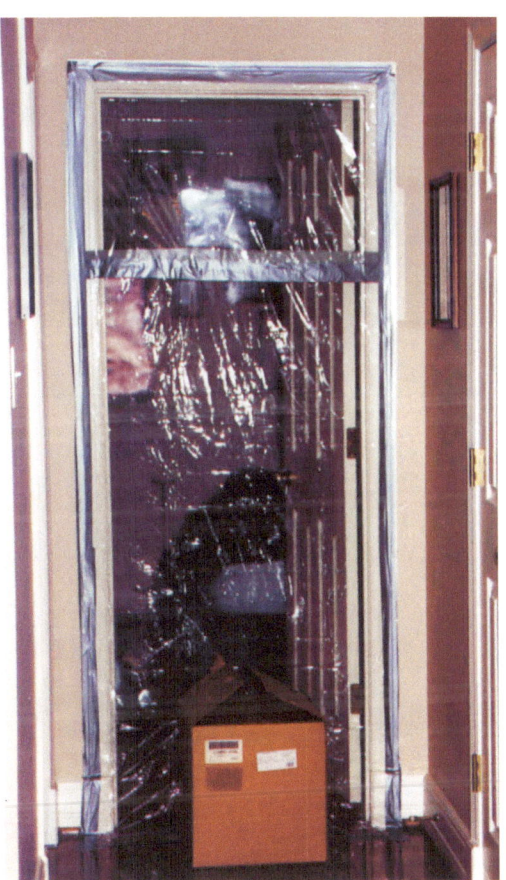

Photo 9.

Step 10.  Connect foot pump and or battery pump to air filter.

Cut a small hole in the back of the box which is the same size as the foot pump hose. If necessary, cut off any plastic tabs or protrusions that may be on the end of the hose. Stick the hose into the hole and seal around the juncture with tape. Attach the other end of the hose to the side marked deflate on the foot pump. Next you will need to seal the box shut with some more packaging or duct tape.

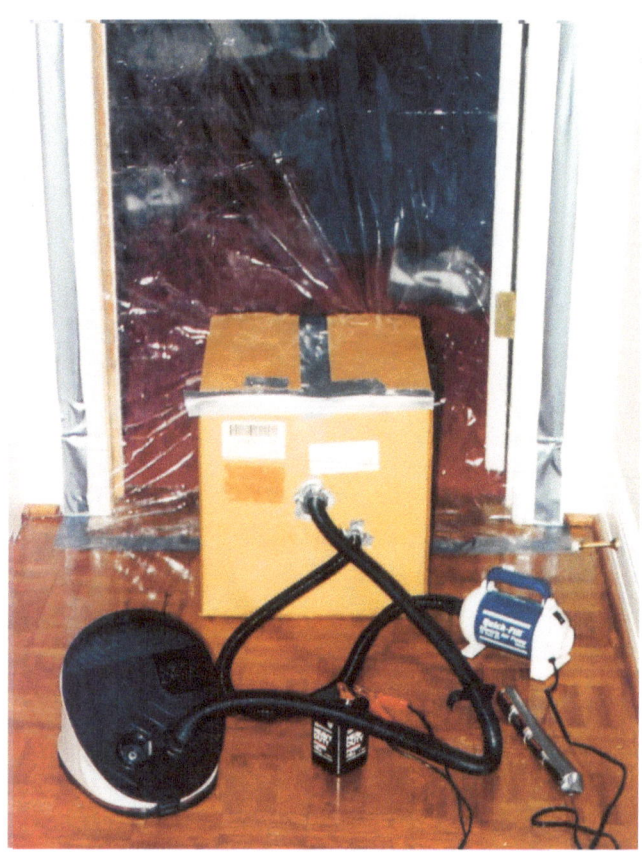

Photo 10.

## Section 4
## Powering The  Air Filtration System

I have experimented with three ways to power the air filtration box and found that the two best devices are the foot powered air pump, available at sporting goods stores  and the 12 volt air pump by  Intex, which is designed to work with an auto battery. The foot pump can pull about 1.25 cubic feet of air per minute through the filter box and into the room. There are several different ways in which the pump can be used with little effort besides the  foot method. For instance, while kneeling on a pillow, you can depress the pump with your arm or with your other knee. By rocking back and forth side ways you can depress the pump with very little effort. The advantage to this pump is that it doesn't require any external energy source such as batteries but the disadvantage is that it takes effort to use.

To use the Intex 12 volt pump, I cut the cigarette adapter off the end, separated the two wires for about a one foot length and stripped the black plastic coating from the end of the wires for about an inch. I attached alligator clips to each wire and was then ready to use any kind of battery I could find. Easy attach alligator clips can be found at Radio Shack and the Walmart auto dept. Remove the plastic sheath from the alligator clip and slip it over the wire end (It didn't matter which wire went to which clip). Thread the bare wire end through the protruding loop and twist it as you would a picture frame wire. (See photo 11a). Fold the tabs at the base around the wire, slide the plastic sheath back over the clip and then repeat the procedure for the other clip.

After attaching the clips I was able to operate the pump using my auto battery in addition to, A, C, and D size batteries plus, a 6 volt lantern battery. To use the small batteries I just lined them up in a row, taped them together, taped one alligator clip to the end and turned it off and on by touching the other clip to the other end of the line of Batteries. (See photo 11b)

Attached to an auto battery, the Intex pump was able to pull 9.5 cubic feet per minute through the filter box and lasted longer than 6 hours. When it was powered by a 6 volt lantern battery my Intex pump pulled 2.5 cubic feet per minute through my filter box and ran for about 2 hours. Never allow more than 2 cubic feet per minute to pass through any one filter as this is too fast to allow the air to be purified. This means that If you plan to use an auto battery and the Intex pump you should use five filters in your filter box regardless of the number of people in your shelter. In section 8, Living In Your Shelter we'll deal with how much air to bring into your shelter and how to adjust for the Intex rapid pumping speed.

After you have constructed your filter box as shown in photo10 you can test the sealing job you did using the clove oil. Install the filter in a doorway with yourself on the inside and a helper on the outside. Have your helper put some oil on a tissue or rag and wave it in front of the filter box while it is in use. If you are able to smell cloves then one or more seals is leaking. You should reseal them and test it again.

Photo 11a     Photo 11b     Photo 11c

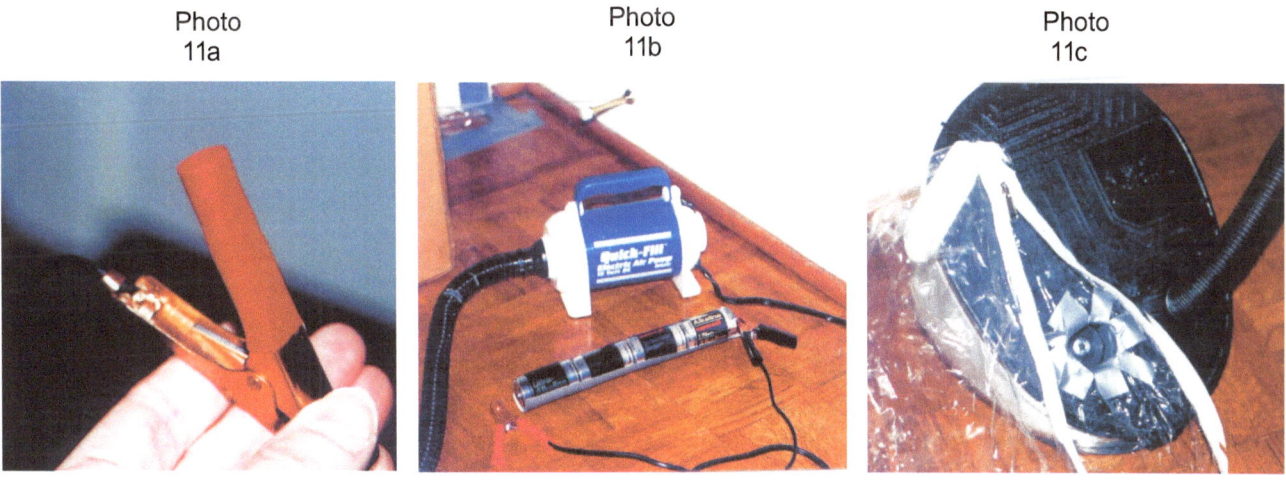

# Section 5
## Constructing an Isolation Room

### CHOOSING THE APPROPRIATE ROOM

The season of the year, the type of toxin, the ease of sealing, and size will all determine your choice of room. Since you will be turning off all power to your house at your circuit breaker, the outside temperature must also be considered when choosing the room. A bathroom can never be sealed adequately because of its plumbing and therefore must be excluded completely.

Only in a nuclear attack will the mass of your walls be a factor. In that case, the basement or partial basement room is best. The next best would be brick and last would be wood siding. In mid summer you should pick the coolest room and in winter the room with the best sun exposure. Of all these factors, size may be the most important factor for you. Due to carbon dioxide build-up, the largest room will allow you to remain in isolation for the longest time. We'll talk about air requirements in Section 8. Since your only light source will be battery powered, having at least one outside window will be necessary and if that window is opposite the door you will establish better air circulation. At the other end of the spectrum, a room that is all windows and doors would be less desirable unless it was draft free and could be totally covered with plastic.

If at all possible you should decide in advance which rooms of your home are the potential candidates and then cut out pieces of plastic that would fit over those windows in advance. The cut sheets can be stored away in the air filtration box.

### MAKING A COMPLETE SEAL

Windows and doors are not the only places where outside air can get into your space. To make a complete seal you will need to cover and seal all the electrical outlets, light switches, light fixtures, heat and air ducts, and any other openings or cracks where air might seep in. Before tampering with light fixtures, however, be sure to turn off your power at the circuit breaker. If you have taped the plastic sheeting which contains the air filtration box directly to the door trim, you will need to check for gaps where the door trim overlaps the wallboard. Seal over any cracks with duct tape.

To seal the outlets, cut plastic 3-6 inches bigger than the wall plate and tape to the wall on all sides with duct tape. Next, cut and tape plastic over all windows, allowing 6-8 inches of overlap around the outside to accommodate the window sills. Be sure to leave one of the covered windows just slightly cracked, as later, you will be providing an escape outlet for excess air. After checking that the power supply is off, remove any ceiling fixtures which are too large to cover with plastic and seal the hole as you did the windows. Cover over any heating and air ducts or air returns and any other openings where air can leak in. Remember that your goal is to allow no air into your shelter except through the filters in the air filtration box.

The last and most difficult feature to seal are the baseboards. If the room you have chosen as your shelter has wall to wall carpeting this may be a tedious task. First you will need to pull the carpet up from the floor around the edges of the room. If it's possible to get duct tape between the base board and the carpet strip all the better. But if the carpet strip is so close to the baseboard that you can't make a good seal you will have to seal over the entire thing. (See figure 2.)  Covering the nails with a thin strip of cardboard the same width as the tack strip will prevent the nails from puncturing the tape.

An alternative way to tackle the problem would be to use caulk and apply it liberally to the area circled. Seal around the entire room. A third way which might be possible would be to cover the entire floor and baseboard with plastic sheeting.

Sealing an entire room as described can be too big a job to do in a hurry, but if necessary, the smaller, more difficult to seal leaks, can be tackled after you are sealed inside your shelter and are pumping in filtered air.

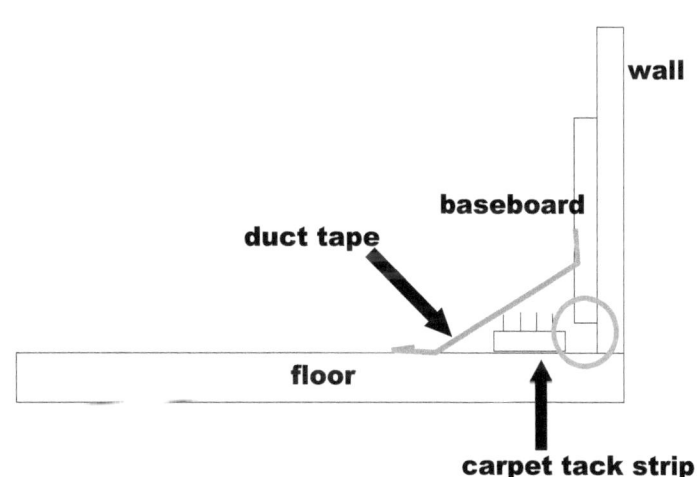

Figure 2.

# Section 6
## Provisions

Once you have made plans for providing clean air for your family, you can begin to look at the other things that will be necessary to sustain health and life; food, water and hygiene.

## FOOD

Once you have sealed up your shelter you will no longer be able to prepare cooked meals. In addition to this constraint, the foods you take into your shelter will have to be mostly dry and canned. With both constraints your diet will be less than thrilling, however, good planning can make it nutritious and filling. Since most foods lose nutritional value over time, it would not be a good idea to buy food and then stash it away in a closet for what may be 10 years or hopefully forever. The best way to handle this is to try to always keep a large supply on hand but rotate foods by date so that you will have a good supply of recently dated foods on hand at all times.

Keep on hand a variety of canned meats, vegetables and fruit. Dry fruit, crackers, canned beans, evaporated milk, and olive oil are some other good things to have around as are vitamins and minerals.

## WATER

Based on a water requirement of 2 qts/person/day, a family of four would require 14 gallons over a 1 week period. This requirement is for drinking water only and doesn't take into account water needs for washing. If you are able to keep water stored in empty 2 liter bottles, they would be the most stable plastic container for liquids. Keeping them around and filled, however, is problematic. If it isn't possible to get bottles or get them filled in time I wouldn't hesitate to line my waste baskets with several layers of plastic trash bags and fill the bags with water. Normally it wouldn't be advisable to store drinking water in a container which wasn't designed for that use, however, in a life or death situation you have to weigh the relative risks. Water purification tablets are available at sporting goods stores and over the internet and should be included in your supplies.

## HYGIENE

At best bathing will be limited to washcloth rubdowns, but since any water that is left over has to be stored, it would be better to use baby wetwipes. Try to keep enough wipes on hand to provide 1 to 3 per person per day for at least three days.

Toilet facilities will be the old fashioned chamber pot. If your room has a clothes closet, you can remove its contents and make it into a temporary toilet. Porta potty chemicals are available at sporting goods stores and will make it possible to deal safely with human waste for a long period of time.

## POTASSIUM IODIDE

Nuclear experts recommend taking a 10 day course of potassium iodide immediately following a nuclear event. This prevents the thyroid gland from absorbing radioactive iodine which is especially harmful to children. These pills and dosage information are available on the internet at ki4u.com/#5.

# Section 7
## Planning for Last Minute Preparations

While some family members are moving supplies into the room you have chosen, someone else should be making last minute preparations for isolation. If you have not already done so, you should turn the house power off by pulling the main circuit breaker. Turn off your water and gas supplies, if possible. If time allows, open your refrigerator and freezer doors and dump your perishable foods into a plastic bag and seal it.

Before this point, however, you should have made an important crisis management decision. If you think that minutes are going to be critical and you don't expect to be in isolation for more than a day, then you should gather only the provisions and supplies you think you will need for that time period. Turn off your electricity, seal the doorway opening and begin pulling air through the air filtration box immediately. You can finish sealing the windows and other openings after you have sealed the doorway. If, on the other hand, you think you may have a day or so before being exposed to nuclear fallout, you can take time to gather supplies for a longer isolation and check your shelter for leaks.

Take special note that the damage done to your body by nuclear fallout and warfare chemicals is proportional to the amount of the substance that gets into your system. This means that even if you believe you have already breathed some non- biological toxic substance, you should go ahead with isolation plans anyway. Lessening your body's total exposure can be as worthy a goal as preventing exposure. If there is a possibility that your clothing has been contaminated, you should consider changing into clean clothes and sealing the contaminated clothes inside plastic bags.

Ultimately the individual preparation plans you make should have a great deal to do with where you live. For instance, if you live well away from a major city you would probably be most concerned with nuclear fallout, however, if you live in a major city and expect a sophisticated attack from a superpower nation, you would be concerned with all of the types of NBC warfare. For those in cities, having the ability to flee from your home while wearing an NBC mask might be more desirable than remaining in a shelter, but on the other hand, massive chaos in the streets might make you safer remaining inside. If you can afford to have both capabilities, you would offer yourself the greatest flexibility and safety. In any case, these are the sorts of things you should think about and plan for in advance because your individual situation is different from anyone else's.

# Section 8
## Living In Your Shelter

Once you have moved into your shelter you will be adjusting to very different and difficult conditions than you are used to. The fresh, filtered air you will bring into your shelter will be enough to sustain your life but not enough to keep you comfortable. You may become insufferably hot or cold, but thinking of your own or your children's health for the rest of their lives may allow you to persevere in spite of the hardship. The amount of time you can spend in your shelter is determined by the amount of carbon dioxide being produced by your shelter party, the size of your shelter room and how much airflow you can bring into your shelter room. If you expect to need several days of confinement, then regulating the use of battery power to match your minimum needs is crucial.

Controlling your air supply:
If you have bought both a foot pump and the 12 volt dc air pump you will have more flexibility for getting clean air into your shelter. The advantage of the foot pump is that it doesn't require batteries while the advantage of the Intex 12 volt air pump is that it can be modified to run on most any kind of battery.

To determine if you can use the foot pump only, use the following chart to compute your fresh air requirements:

Breathing Volumes

| | |
|---|---|
| Adult Male or young man | 6.0 liters/minute = .22 ft$^3$/minute |
| Adult Female | 4.5 liters/minute = .16 ft$^3$/minute |
| Child | 3.0 liters/minute = .11 ft$^3$/minute |

For a family comprised of a father, mother, teenage son, and two children, you would add .22+.16+.22+.11+.11=.82 cubic feet per minute. Then **double** this number to determine the optimum air flow. The Sevylor model 304 foot pump shown in the photograph of supplies pulls approximately .067 cubic feet of air with each compression cycle. If you use a different type of foot pump then you should determine for yourself how much air is pulled through with each compression*. I was easily able to pump 1.25 cubic feet of air per minute using my Sevylor foot pump but that is a little less than the desirable 1.64 cubic feet I would want to provide for this hypothetical family. To offset this deficiency I would pump for one or two minutes with my battery powered pump, aiming for an average over ten to twenty minutes of the 1.64 cubic feet per minute. By making two holes in the filtration box you can attach both devices to the box at the same time which will save you the trouble of switching hoses to the box when you change devices. (Photo 10)

\* See Appendix for instructions on measuring pump volume

The preceding calculations are based on averages and may not reflect your actual air requirements. Muscular people may demand more oxygen and obese people less. Smokers and people with respiratory diseases will also require a greater volume of air supplied to them. These calculations are also based on persons at rest. You should use the chart as a general guideline but let your bodies be your final guide. Your body will let you know if you are not getting enough air, in which case you should pump more frequently or increase the amount of time you run your air pump per hour.

The reason air is specified and not oxygen is because you are more likely to suffer from elevated levels of carbon dioxide than you are to suffer from a lack of oxygen. To give you a better understanding of respiration, the following chart will be helpful.

Percent Concentrations of Respiratory Gasses*

|  | Atmospheric Air | Humidified Air | Expired Air |
| --- | --- | --- | --- |
| $N_2$ | 78.62% | 74.09% | 74.5% |
| $O_2$ | 20.84% | 19.67% | 15.7% |
| $CO_2$ | 0.04% | 0.04% | 3.6% |
| $H_2O$ | 0.50% | 6.2% | 6.2% |

*Warning! You must not stop pumping or pump any less often than the required pumping as death may occur.*

As long as carbon dioxide levels remain under about 2.0% there will be no adverse physiological effects on your party. If, however, members of your party begin yawning, this signals a buildup of carbon dioxide and you should pump more frequently and those people should move closer to the pump. As an interesting aside, you can reduce your body's carbon dioxide production by 15% by eating only calories from fat, however, ingesting large amounts of oil would probably cause diarrhea.

For every liter of air you pump into your shelter you will need to provide a way for a liter of air to leave. If the large sheet of plastic in the doorway is not pushed outward then leaks somewhere in your shelter are allowing the pumped air to escape and you don't know for sure that outside air is not entering. Ideally, you want the plastic sheet to be bowed out only slightly, which will allow you to control the volume of exiting air by puncturing some pin holes in the plastic sheeting which is placed over the window. Group the holes close together over the area where the window is cracked and be ready to quickly cover them with duct tape if you notice the air is not going out through them. This will require one person to be responsible for watching and regulating the air flow out of the shelter. Another person should be checking all the seals in the room at regular intervals to be sure none are coming loose.

*
**Figures from "Textbook of Medical Physiology", Arthur C. Guyton, 1976**

Latrine:
Plastic garbage bags, cardboard boxes and porta potty chemicals will make it possible to deal with sewage for a very long time. A plastic bucket can make a good temporary potty as would a camper's or boater's porta potty; if you only use it for urine. The reason for not using it for feces is that you won't have the water required for flushing. Since you have to severely limit your washing and cleaning, it would be advantageous to keep urine and feces separate until you put them into your storage receptacle. The receptacle is simply a cardboard box which is lined with 3 or 4 layers of sturdy plastic garbage bags. Empty a packet of porta potty chemicals into the garbage bag, add urine to it and close with a twist-tie. By having BMs on heavy duty paper towels, the waste can be more easily transferred to the plastic bag. Latex and nonlatex disposable gloves are available and  would be useful in making this transfer. To avoid opening and closing the garbage bag receptacle every time someone uses the toilet, you may want to store the paper-towel wrapped BMs and dirty toilet paper in quart size ziplock bags until evening at which time you can deposit all that have accumulated.

Be careful to avoid any foods that cause you to have loose stools. Recently, sterilizing wipes have been offered for sale and would be well suited for hand washing. Liquid hand sanitizer is also available from several soap companies. You can soak paper towels in the liquid hand sanitizer to make your own sterile wipes.

Food preparation:
The variety of meals you can prepare will be severely limited by the lack of variety of foods available, the lack of cooking heat, and the lack of cleanup facilities. Still, you will have access to and control over more food than you would have had in a refugee shelter.

Try to dirty as few containers and utensils as possible, eating directly from the cans when possible. For cleanups, a sterile wet wipe and a slightly damp paper towel would work well. Dispose of used paper plates and plastic utensils in Ziplock bags in order to isolate any disease producing organisms.

# Section 9
# System Limitations

## CARBON DIOXIDE

As previously mentioned, failure to continue pumping fresh air into your shelter at the rate specified will likely result in severe respiratory distress or the deaths of yourself and your entire shelter group. If you find yourself in the middle of the night, too sleepy to continue operating the pump and no one else will relieve you from pump duty you would serve your group better by unsealing your doorway and breathing the house air while you sleep. Remember that reducing your total exposure to low levels of toxic substances is also a worthwhile goal. Depending on air quality reports which may be  broadcast, you might decide to reseal your doorway after you wake up. If you are only using a foot pump, under no circumstances should you allow yourself to think that you can pump harder for a little while, take a short nap and then pump harder after you wake up, as waking up may not come. In consideration of the very great physical burden of air pumping day and night, you should not endeavor to stay overnight in a shelter without at least two healthy and motivated adults to share the burden. Keep in mind that the first physiological effect of rising concentrations of carbon dioxide are yawning and deep heavy breathing. Shelter occupants who are breathing in too much $CO_2$ will breathe heavily and rapidly until the concentration of carbon dioxide passes 9 percent. Above this level, unconsciousness, coma and then death will occur.

## FILTER LIMITATIONS

Whether you use military NBC filters or any other type filters, you will be using a product which can be used up and then is no longer effective. On the plus side, the NBC filters have been designed to protect the user even in high concentrations of toxins for up to a few hours. The in-home shelter plan relies on the expectation that these toxic substances will be substantially diluted by the time they reach your shelter. This will allow you to use the filters for a much longer time.

If you think that your geographical location and political situation put you at a greater risk than most, you should construct a backup filter bank which could be taped in place behind the first bank when you believe the first set of filters are spent. One way of knowing that the filters are spent would be the transmission of odors from outside your shelter. If the incoming air has any odor at all then the filters are no longer functional. A backup filter bank is simply a duplicate of the side of the filter box that contains the filters, but not the plastic sheeting. Simply open up the box from the top, set the second filter bank about 2 inches behind the first set of filters, tape the filter bank to the bottom, sides and top flap of the box and then reseal the top of the box. Air will still pass through the first set of filters but will be filtered by the second set.

When using the foot pump be careful to control the speed at which air is pulled through the filters at the beginning of each deflate  cycle. In other words, don't allow the spring to have complete control over the pulling speed as too fast an airflow through the filters will lessen their effectiveness.

# SUPPLY LIST

The following supply list can be a shopping list and the check list you can use before sealing your shelter. More important supplies are tagged with a *.

*6mil clear plastic or vinyl ☐ ☐ Shower curtains or roll plastic
To cover openings
*2 rolls packaging tape ☐ ☐
*4 to 6 rolls duct tape ☐ ☐
*Sturdy box plus 4 other boxes ☐ ☐
*Battery operated air pump ☐ ☐
*Alligator clips ☐ ☐ Organic vapot paint filters if only option
*NBC filters (1 or 2 per person) ☐ ☐
*Sevlor foot operated air pump ☐ ☐ Sporting goods stores
*Porta Potty chemicals ☐ ☐
*100 quart sized ziplock bags ☐ ☐
*Tool to remove auto battery ☐ ☐
^Auto battery ☐ ☐
*Any other batteries ☐ ☐
*50 plastic trash bags ☐ ☐
*2 plastic buckets ☐ ☐
 Toilet seat from toilet ☐ ☐ Optional
*Tool to remove carpet tacks ☐ ☐ Optional tool box
*Sharp kieves ☐ ☐
*Toilet paper ☐ ☐

*Kleenex ☐ ☐
*Ultra heavy paper towels ☐ ☐
*2 quarts high proof liquor ☐ ☐ For sterilization
 Instant coffee ☐ ☐ Optional
 Canned milk ☐ ☐
^Canned vegetables ☐ ☐
*Canned green beans ☐ ☐
*Canned meat ☐ ☐
*Spices, salt, pepper ☐ ☐
 Olive or canola oil ☐ ☐
*Crackers etc. ☐ ☐
 Vitamins ☐ ☐
*Plastic silverware ☐ ☐
*Plastic cups ☐ ☐
*Paper plates ☐ ☐
*Can opener ☐ ☐
*Water ☐ ☐ .5X(#persons)X(days in shelter)=_____gal.
*Water purification tablets ☐ ☐ Sporting goods stores
 Blankets, pillows ☐ ☐
 Sheets ☐ ☐

*Toothbrushes ☐ ☐
*Toothpaste ☐ ☐
*Wetwipes 160/person ☐ ☐
Battery radio ☐ ☐
*Cellphone ☐ ☐
*Batteries ☐ ☐
*Flashlight ☐ ☐
*Whistle ☐ ☐
*Bible ☐ ☐
*5liquor store boxes ☐ ☐
*Scissors ☐ ☐
*Paper ☐ ☐
*Pencil or pen ☐ ☐
*Calculator ☐ ☐
Sleeping bags ☐ ☐
Air mattresses ☐ ☐
Bath soap ☐ ☐
Deodorant ☐ ☐
Cloth towels ☐ ☐

## FIRST AID

*Thermometer ☐ ☐
*Bandages ☐ ☐
*Rubbing alcohol ☐ ☐
*Tylenol ☐ ☐
*Aspirin ☐ ☐
*Ibuprofen ☐ ☐
*Medicines you need ☐ ☐
*Potassium iodide ☐ ☐

## LAST MINUTE PRECAUTIONS

Turn off gas ☐ ☐
Turn off electric ☐ ☐
Turn off water ☐ ☐

Here are just a few of many websites offering disaster equipment;

www.ki4u.com
(Potassium Iodide tablets and info.)

www.imsplus.com/ims29.html
(gas masks and accessories)

Quartermaster
Www.qm-supply.com
(NBC filters)

Since the following calculations may be difficult to complete if you are under stress, I highly recommend that you record measurements for your equipment in this book before you store your filter box away. If, however, you haven't measured in advance you shouldn't panic but simply begin pumping at a comfortable speed and let someone else help you with calculations. You do have a large reserve of good air inside your room which will give you some room for errors at the beginning of your isolation.

The easiest way to determine the amount of air your pumping devices can move through your filter box is to prepare a plastic measuring bag. To make this bag you can use any kind of rectangular, clear plastic linen bag which has a zipper. These are the kind of bag that blankets and mattress pads come packaged in. Cut about a one and a half inch hole in the narrow flap which the zipper surrounds. With the bag opened, and working from the inside of the bag, fit the hole over the air exit hole on the foot pump or 12 volt pump and tape it in place using some small pieces of duct tape. (Photo 11c, pg.18) Next you should flatten the bag as much as you can and close the zipper. Seal over the zipper with some more duct tape, remembering that you want the bag as empty of air as possible.

Foot Pump:

If the filter box is attached to the foot pump, simply begin pumping air into the bag while counting the number of pumps it takes to fill the bag. Use the following formulas to compute your pumping rate. For example, If it took 15 pumps to fill the bag:

MULTIPLY  in inches (length of bag) times (width of bag) times (height of bag) Divide this number by 1728 to get the volume of the bag in cubic feet.
For example;

$$(15in) X (18in) X (4in) = 1080$$

$$\frac{1080}{1728} = .625 \text{ cubic feet in 15 pumps of the foot pump}$$

Your bag size  $\dfrac{\rule{2cm}{0.4pt}}{1728} =$

Next you need to measure the number of compressions you can easily make in a minute. For example, if this number was 19, multiply the pumps per minute times the size of the bag and divide this number by the number of pumps it took to fill the bag.

$$\frac{19 \times .625}{15} = .79 \text{ cubic feet per minute}$$

$$\frac{\rule{2cm}{0.4pt}}{} = \qquad \text{Your cubic feet per minute}$$

12 Volt Pump:

Remember to use a minimum of 5 filters in your box if you use an auto battery for power. With the measuring bag attached to the 12 volt pump, fill the bag again while counting the seconds it takes to fill. For instance; if it takes 10 seconds to fill the bag, make the following calculation using the same number you got for the size of the bag in cubic feet ( .625 cubic feet).  Multiply the cubic feet times 60 and divide by the number of seconds it took to fill the bag. For example:

$$\frac{.625 \times 60}{10} = 3.75 \text{ cubic feet per minute}$$

Record your
measurements          —————          =
here

## PERFORM THE FOLLOWING CALCULATIONS
## TO DETERMINE HOW LONG TO RUN THE BATTERY PUMP

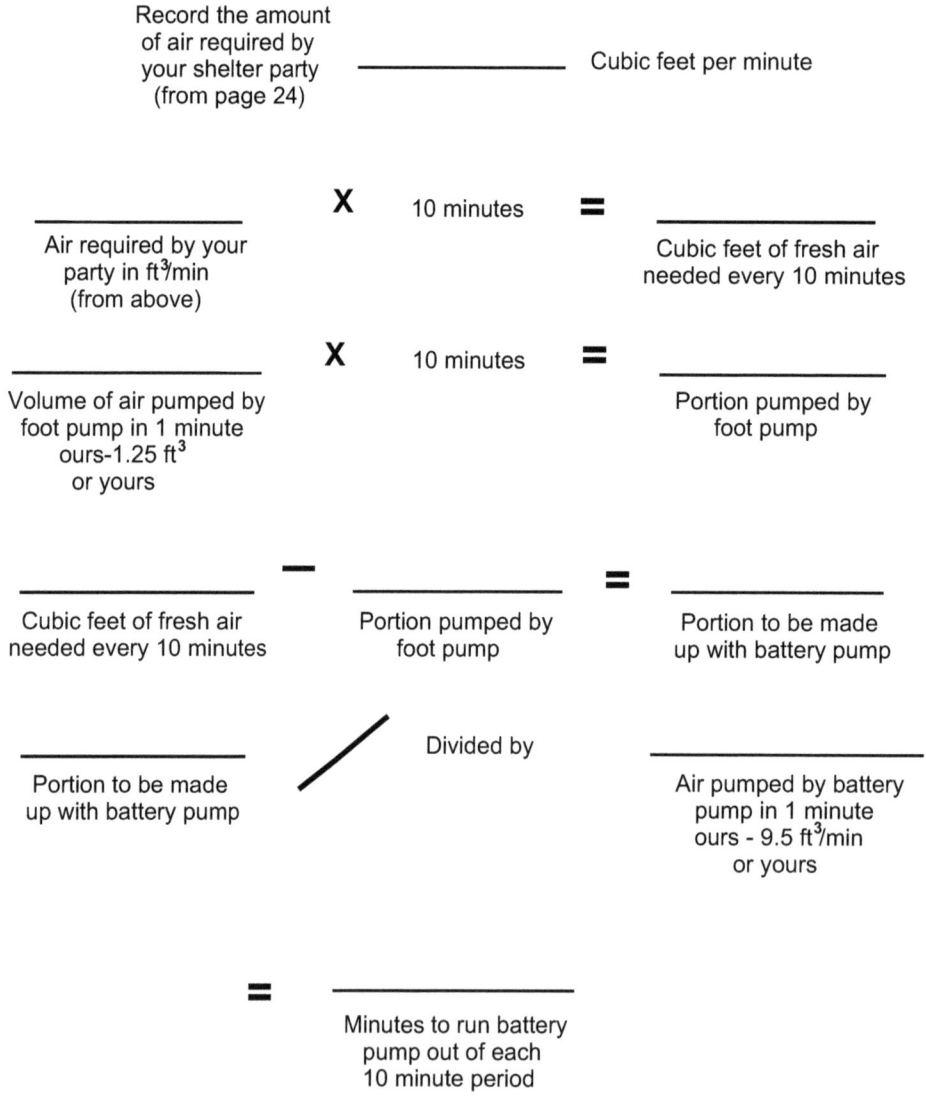

Record the amount
of air required by
your shelter party          —————————          Cubic feet per minute
(from page 24)

_____     **X**     10 minutes     **=**     _____
Air required by your                                   Cubic feet of fresh air
party in ft³/min                                       needed every 10 minutes
(from above)

_____     **X**     10 minutes     **=**     _____
Volume of air pumped by                                Portion pumped by
foot pump in 1 minute                                  foot pump
ours-1.25 ft³
or yours

_____     **—**     _____     **=**     _____
Cubic feet of fresh air          Portion pumped by          Portion to be made
needed every 10 minutes          foot pump                  up with battery pump

_____     /     Divided by          _____
Portion to be made                                     Air pumped by battery
up with battery pump                                   pump in 1 minute
ours - 9.5 ft³/min
or yours

**=**     _____
Minutes to run battery
pump out of each
10 minute period

September 10, 2016

Dear Reader,

I would like to be able to offer this product ready-made as a fully engineered and industry-approved product. Of course, the price would be determined by the demand.

If you would be interested in buying the filtration box and air pump ready-made with the best possible materials, gaskets, seals etc. Please email me at mmdwmd@gmail.com. Letting me know what you would be willing to pay for the system would help me towards my goal of offering affordable protection for all people.

Thanks Very Much,

Malcolm McDaniel

www.ingramcontent.com/pod-product-compliance
Lightning Source LLC
Chambersburg PA
CBHW060807290526
45792CB00005BA/1557